Advance Praise for the new Penguin Poets edition of

# THE SONNETS

### *by Ted Berrigan*

"*The Sonnets* is a poetic dynamo that has inspired poets and energized readers of poetry ever since its initial publication in 1964. Beautifully introduced and annotated by Alice Notley, this new edition of Ted Berrigan's masterpiece is the definitive one, the one to have, the one to marvel at."
—Ron Padgett

"*The Sonnets* has been an ur-text for generations of experimental writing. Sinewy disjuncts, sharp amalgams of quote and wit, shifting identities, *The Sonnets* are frolics for the rhizomic reader. How generous Berrigan's mind in all ten directions at once, his romantic latitudes. The New York School has been well served by one of its radiant and prodigious sons."
—Anne Waldman

"Part collage, part process writing, part sprung lyric, Ted Berrigan's *The Sonnets* remains, almost forty years after its composition, one of the freshest and most buoyantly inspired works of contemporary poetry. Reinventing verse for its time, *The Sonnets* are redolent with possibilities for our own."
—Charles Bernstein

"Berrigan's words often seem to be taking his ideas on a very brisk outing, from which they return with flushed cheeks and euphoria in their lungs. More, perhaps, than any of his colleagues, Berrigan has converted poetry into an environment."
—John Ashbery

"*The Sonnets* remains one of the most exciting books of poetry of the last half century. Berrigan's collage and recombination continually open the door to giddy discovery and the deepest comedy. This book dispels the solemnity and anti-inventiveness which all too often surround poetry. A glance inside will reveal how poetry acts when it's alive."
—Bob Perelman

# THE SONNETS

## Ted Berrigan

*Introduction by Alice Notley*

PENGUIN POETS

PENGUIN BOOKS
Published by the Penguin Group
Penguin Putnam Inc., 375 Hudson Street,
New York, New York 10014, U.S.A.
Penguin Books Ltd, 27 Wrights Lane,
London W8 5TZ, England
Penguin Books Australia Ltd, Ringwood,
Victoria, Australia
Penguin Books Canada Ltd, 10 Alcorn Avenue,
Toronto, Ontario, Canada M4V 3B2
Penguin Books (N.Z.) Ltd, 182–190 Wairau Road,
Auckland 10, New Zealand

Penguin Books Ltd, Registered Offices:
Harmondsworth, Middlesex, England

This edition first published in Penguin Books 2000

1 3 5 7 9 10 8 6 4 2

Some of the poems appeared in "C" (A Journal of Poetry); Locus Solus V; Art & Literature; The Paris Review;
Kulchur; Captain May I; and in An Anthology of New York Poets; The Norton Anthology of Poetry; America,
A Prophecy; The East Side Scene; Acid (Martz Books, Cologne); Giovani Poeti Americani (Rome); and in the
following books by Ted Berrigan: Many Happy Returns (Corinth Books, New York, 1967); Guillaume
Apollinaire Ist Tot (Marz Books, Cologne, 1971); Red Wagon (Yellow Press, Chicago, 1975); Nothing
For You (United Artists, New York, 1977); So Going Around Cities (Blue Wind, Berkeley, 1980).

LIBRARY OF CONGRESS CATALOGING-IN-PUBLICATION DATA
Berrigan, Ted.
    The sonnets / Ted Berrigan ; introduction by Alice Notley.
    p.    cm.
    Includes bibliographical references (p.    ).
    ISBN 0-14-058927-9
    1. Sonnets, American. I. Title.

PS3552.E74 S6 2000
811'.54—dc21        00-027865

Printed in the United States of America
Set in Weiss
Designed by Ellen Cipriano

# INTRODUCTION

■

According to Ted Berrigan, in an unpublished manuscript called "Speaking Of Picasso . . ." and dated "5 March 82," *The Sonnets* was written in March, April and May of 1963 when the author was twenty-eight years old. There were originally eighty-eight sonnets, and though they are, in fact, a sequence in the classical, or at least the Shakespearean sense, each one is also intended to stand alone.

The above dates are substantially correct, though *The Sonnets* incorporates poems and parts of poems written in the earlier 1960s and in the late 1950s. One of its themes is time, the incorporation of the past into the present becoming the future, and so each sonnet seems to have invisible arrows pointing out from it backwards, forwards, and sideways too, creating a long complex moment that certain manuscripts of Ted's tell us is most literally the spring of 1963. Ted always used to say that *The Sonnets* has a plot very like Shakespeare's *Sonnets* involving friendships and triangular love relationships; but where Shakespeare's plot is patterned chronologically Ted's is patterned simultaneously, and where Shakespeare's story is overt Ted's is buried beneath a surface of names, repetitions, and fragmented experience that in this age seem more like life than a bald story does. *The Sonnets* was written by a young man in a period of intense self-education and self-development, but it embodies change in a form that's solid and even monumental. It's about friends and loves but it's also about painting, music, architecture, philosophy, novels, the movies, and cultural icons: it's about life becoming art and what that feels and looks like, literally; it's tactile and blocklike and covered with finely carved motifs.

Ted was born in Providence, Rhode Island, in 1934, of working-class parents. He attended a Catholic academy in Providence and then passed a year at Providence College, also a Catholic institution, in a state of trance, he always said. In 1954 at the age of nineteen he enlisted in the army in order to get out of Providence and find a different sort of life. He seems to have had no idea at that time that he would become a poet. He served eighteen months in Korea and then twelve months in Tulsa; when his tour of duty was over he stayed on in Tulsa to attend the University of Tulsa under the GI Bill. Then he began to meet people, young poets like Dick Gallup, and Ron Padgett, who was editing *The White Dove Review* while still in high school, publishing work by writers like Jack Kerouac (Ursula Le Guin was a subscriber). He also met the artist Joe Brainard, to whom *The Sonnets* would be dedicated. He wrote his first poems and published a first chapbook, the notoriously sentimental *A Lily For My Love*, as many copies as possible of which he later tried to destroy. He received a B.A. in English in 1959 and then began an M.A., but moved to New York in 1961, returning to Tulsa in 1962 just long enough to complete the oral examinations for his M.A. His master's thesis, "The Problem Of How To Live As Dealt With In Four Plays By George Bernard Shaw," had already been accepted.

Ted lived in New York now, always below Fourteenth Street, in that Greenwich Village/Lower East Side ambiance of immigrants, writers and artists, small stores and dirt and bright sunlight. A lot of friends from Tulsa had also moved to New York: Dick, Ron, Joe, and, among others, Pat Mitchell who was to become Pat Padgett, and the flautist Anne Kepler. The latter two are Patsy and Anne in *The Sonnets*, though Patsy is also sometimes Patsy Nicholson, a Tulsan who stayed in Tulsa. There are denizens of *The Sonnets* who are not former Tulsans but people who came to New York from elsewhere: for example, Carol Clifford who was a little later Carol Gallup, and Sandra Alper who became Ted's first wife Sandy Berrigan. All these names play across the book as well as names specific only to Tulsa and the years Ted had lived in Tulsa: Chris, who was Chris Murphy, a junior high school student; Margie Kepler, a nurse and also Anne Kepler's cousin; Bernie, Pat Mitchell's sister; Bearden, Martin Cochran, etc. Pat, Carol, Anne, and Margie were all women with whom Ted had been romantically involved; his girlfriends often later became his friends. Chris, the mysterious muse of *The Sonnets*, remained sealed up in a single year's friendship and was a sort of Beatrice, someone very young with whom contact was severed. Intertwined with the names of lovers and friends are the names of poets and artists and musicians and "figures": Frank O'Hara, John Ashbery, Guillaume Apollinaire, William Carlos Williams, Jackson Pollock, Gus Cannon, Lonnie Johnson, Gertrude Stein, Ford Madox Ford, Marilyn Monroe, Billy the Kid, Francis Marion, Benedict Arnold, and so on. It's a pantheon of Modernists and Postmodernists, boyhood heroes, and people representing a new American sensibility— the blues musicians, for instance. It's both classical and eclectic, as *The Sonnets* itself is.

How did Ted manage to change from being the poet of *A Lily For My Love* to the author of *The Sonnets*? As hinted above, the process of that change is incorporated into the book. There had been crucial life changes: dissolution of certain relationships and formation of others, the move to New York, certain traumas pointed to but not entirely delineated in *The Sonnets*:

> I never thought on the Williams-
> burg bridge I'd come so much to Brooklyn
> just to see lawyers and cops who don't even carry
> guns taking my wife away and bringing her back . . .

> (Sonnet XXXVI)

Ted had also discovered the poems of Frank O'Hara and John Ashbery, the theories of John Cage, the philosophy of Alfred North Whitehead, and the works of the Dadaists and Surrealists; and he and Joe Brainard together were taking in Art in New York. Pollock was recently dead, deKooning in his prime, Warhol, Johns, and Rauschenberg young men; the Cubists could be examined at the MOMA; the major Duchamps were nearby in Philadelphia. Joe Brainard himself was beginning to find his own artistic direction: drawings evincing the impeccable line of a cartoonist or commercial artist ("Joe's lettering is getting really good," Andy Warhol once said admiringly to Ted, lettering being a prized skill in the Pop Art sixties) and collages and assemblages composed of meticulously chosen and obviously loved objects: bottles of emeraldine Prell Shampoo, Mexican madonnas, kewpie dolls, feathers, slogan buttons, eyeglasses, costume jewelry, plastic grapes, things chosen for their beauty, and humor, but not for their hipness. Joe also knew how to cut something up into pieces and rearrange it into another mysterious entity that both suggested the identity of the first entity and turned it inside out. In Sonnet XV Ted takes on Joe's expertise and refers to Joe's techniques:

> In Joe Brainard's collage its white arrow
> He is not in it, the hungry dead doctor.
> Of Marilyn Monroe, her white teeth white-
> I am truly horribly upset because Marilyn
> and ate King Korn popcorn," he wrote in his
> of glass in Joe Brainard's collage . . .

But Sonnet XV is a poem, designed to unfold in time, though of course locked up in a still, small place until the reader unfolds it. Its design is literary, not artistic or painterly. It has gotten its literary permissions from certain near predecessors, though it is different from them, and gotten a firm philosophical grounding elsewhere, for this is a remarkably *grounded* poetry. That, as has often been pointed out, each word is bricklike is due to certainty of method and of justification for the method.

The most obvious influence for the disjunctiveness of *The Sonnets* is the poems collected in John Ashbery's *The Tennis Court Oath*; Ted secretly pays tribute to Ezra Pound in Sonnet I and often acknowledged a debt to *The Waste Land*, but they were now far away as to time and place, Europeanized and classically Modernist, not really relevant to 1962, if you were trying to participate in the new American poetry. *The Tennis Court Oath*, published in 1962, contains poems Ashbery wrote in France during a period of linguistic dissociation due to the necessity of living in the French language. They are phrasal, covert, and full of unexpected spaces between lines and thoughts:

scarecrow falls    Time, progress and good sense
strike of shopkeepers dark blood

("Leaving the Atocha Station")

The poems in *The Tennis Court Oath*, though, are not composed to a system, are in different forms, don't reflect a consistency of method only of style. Ted studied them furiously in notebooks now collected at the Lockwood Library at SUNY Buffalo; he scoured them for clues as to sources and meanings and had a theory they were secretly influenced by Sir James Frazer's *The Golden Bough*. At the same time he was seriously marking up John Cage's book *Silence*, first published in 1961. In *Silence* Cage demonstrates the use of aleatory methods of composition, so-called chance methods by which one selects and arranges materials. For example by throwing the I Ching he can determine all the components—pitch, duration, tempo, and so on—of a musical composition. Elsewhere in *Silence* there are lectures on various topics, scored for a four-beat line and laid out in a grid of phrases that must be read, no matter their length, in time to the beat. And other ways of gridding a performance are demonstrated according to which a net, a formal method, conceived apart from the materials themselves, is thrown over them. By 1963, through the agency of Robert Motherwell's *The Dada Painters and Poets: An Anthology*, Ted was also familiar with Tristan Tzara's cutups, poems made from words cut out of newspapers and combined by a chance procedure, and with Hans Arp's chance methods of composing collages. He received from them and from the other Dadaists a respect for the unconscious and in some sense for magic. For Cage, the application of a "method" results in a work or performance that's serene and free, or rather, "liberated," as Cage is a serious Zen Buddhist and his work is permeated with Buddhist thought; for Ted it more results in one that's deeply "true." An aleatory method, used with seriousness and respect, puts one in touch with hidden powers and truths within oneself and becomes revelatory hopefully in a way that might be relevant to anyone. Yet by giving oneself up to chance an artist does not lose his/her originality. As Marcel Duchamp once said, "Your chance is not the same as mine, just as your throw of the dice will rarely be the same as mine." Duchamp had used a chance method to obtain a unit of measurement and shape called the "stoppage," which figures importantly in the painting *Network of Stoppages* and particularly in the *Large Glass*. Duchamp's derivation of the unit, by dropping threads exactly one meter long and tracing their randomly curved lines to make templates, suggests Ted's conception of the line in *The Sonnets* as something that once established becomes rigid in its repetition no matter the syntax involved.

In annotations made in 1982 on a typescript from circa 1962 or '63, Ted repeatedly refers to a "method" or "the method": "the method is similar in all," "Made from Joe's 'secret journal', a prose work, by method," "a method rearrangement," and so on. Ted never really delineated the whole method to anyone, and I think it may be assumed to have been various. In sonnets like XV, it is a mechanical procedure that cannot be violated no matter the outcome. That is, Sonnet XV is an old sonnet of Ted's whose lines have been rearranged according to the formula, line 1, line 14, line 2, line 13, line 3, line 12, and so on in until what was formerly the ending of the poem is now in the middle and vice versa. To do that is to break the ages-old logic of the sonnet and sonnetlike poems and to make a new statement about reality: the outcome or gist of something is in its midst not just at its end. Sonnet XXX is composed of the first lines of the previous fourteen sonnets (according to an earlier, slightly different ordering of the sonnets) arranged according to the same formula as Sonnet XV. Sonnet XXI, on the other hand, which is a rearrangement of all the lines of "Penn Station," is only partly ordered according to that formula, though the presumable goal of turning the poem inside out is still achieved. With most of the poems, though, it's difficult to determine how the materials were chosen and ordered. Some sonnets are composed of phrases, lines, or blocks of material from previous sonnets, exclusively or in combination with new material; some sonnets contain entirely new material; many are composed of lines or blocks of lines from older poems written before *The Sonnets,* or are simply older poems; some are composed of lines by other poets. These poems are pervaded by instincts learned from using chance methods: Ted was searching for what looked unpredicted and what also meant something unpredicted but significant.

The "method" implies that previous units—whole sonnets or sections—are whole in their own time, that is, in their position in the book or standing on their own outside it. But by the rules of the book each new unit will be subject to breakage and reconstitution, as if that were the way time worked, breaking up the elements of experience only to allow their different regrouping later. *The Sonnets* is composed of movable parts, each of which seems to stand for a piece of experience or autobiography, or a knowledge or an opacity, a verbal riddle worth contemplating. Lines and phrases are peculiarly factual entities. Individual lines accumulate more and more weight with their repetition, becoming unforgettable and koanlike. The two lines "In Joe Brainard's collage, there is no such thing / as a breakdown" (XLIII), which themselves combine half of "In Joe Brainard's collage its white arrow" (XV) and "There is no such thing as a breakdown" (XVII), imply that to cut something up into pieces and make something else from them is not to break down the first thing, analyze it, make a portrait of it. The first entity is whole, the second is too, and by extension every sonnet here is whole despite being composed of "pieces." Sonnet XVII, as a matter of fact, is quite explicitly about life's unity and the wholeness of all its manifestations, as in the following lines, where "it" refers to "the pulse of the tree":

> It beats in tiny blots
> Its patternless pattern of excitement
> Letters   birds   beggars   books
> There is no such thing as a breakdown

A subsequent sonnet, LXV, uses the line differently:

Washed by Joe's throbbing hands
She is introspection.
It is a Chinese signal.
There is no such thing as a breakdown

Here the line more takes on the weight of the meaning "nervous break-down," though rather mysteriously. It's not as if someone specific were enduring a breakdown, though someone—"she"—might be. "She" might be Marilyn Monroe, or a lover, or either Joe's or Ted's or both's inward-ness or shakiness or all of the above; nonetheless, "There is no such thing as a breakdown" and that sounds like a credo. Sonnet LXV is in the sec-ond half of the book and so the "plot" has considerably thickened; there have been several shes and there have been hatred, disgust, and betrayal by now, but not attached to specific names, rather attached to specific lines: e.g., "For you I starred in the movie / Made on the site / Of Benedict Arnold's triumph, Ticonderoga . . ." (XXXVIII). Through time, through happenstance, "There is no such thing as a breakdown" has changed its meaning.

How, people sometimes ask, can such sonnets be sonnets? Are they really sonnets, or is *The Sonnets* a "long poem" or a "book"? The book cer-tainly has the feel of a long single work, but the individual poems do also feel like sonnets. Partly that is because they're so firmly gridded to a fourteen-line structure (even though not all of them are fourteen lines long), and partly because they're so slablike and each word so owns its own space; but it's also because the traditional sonnet structure tends to be underneath. There is often the division of the fourteen lines into three four-line groups followed by a couplet, but the transitions between the parts are supple, subtle, and unmarked by rhyme, punctuation, or stanza breaks. Here is Sonnet II:

Dear Margie, hello. It is 5:15 a.m.
dear Berrigan. He died
Back to books. I read

It's 8:30 p.m. in New York and I've been running around all day
old come-all-ye's streel into the streets. Yes, it is now,
How Much Longer Shall I Be Able To Inhabit The Divine
and the day is bright gray turning green
feminine marvelous and tough
watching the sun come up over the Navy Yard
to write scotch-tape body in a notebook
had 17 and 1/2 milligrams
Dear Margie, hello. It is 5:15 a.m.
fucked til 7 now she's late to work and I'm
18 so why are my hands shaking I should know better

The first four lines create a circumstance of letter-writing at dawn, a flash into the future death of the poet, the reading of books, and then a flashback possibly to earlier in the day. The next four lines continue the "description" of the earlier day. The third group of four lines brings the poem back to the dawn atmosphere of the poet still at work at 5:15 a.m. The couplet moves the poem on in time, to "7," but also ends the poem strongly, in the manner of a Shakespearean sonnet. Sonnet II appears to be a list of lines, but the traditional sonnet is also a list of lines. The lines of II are not connected by conjunctions, being pieces of time and circumstance rather than of rhetoric.

There is a key line that occurs only once, in Sonnet L: "Whatever is going to happen is already happening." It refers to Whitehead's theory of time and states quite plainly how *The Sonnets* works, how events are forecast and then ripen, staying on as echoes, or as something built in, through the use of repetition of lines. The line became a sort of motto of Ted's later in life, since it also means "If you aren't doing it now you won't ever do it." It comes from Ted's reading of Whitehead's *Process and Reality*, another book he had heavily annotated. *Process and Reality* contains many passages that seem to point to the ideas behind *The Sonnets*. Of Zeno's "Arrow" paradox and then of his own thought, Whitehead writes: "The conclusion is that in every act of becoming there is the becoming of something with temporal extension; but that the act itself is not extensive, in the sense that it is divisible into earlier and later acts of becoming which correspond to the extensive divisibility of what has become. . . . In this section, the doctrine is enunciated that the creature is extensive, but that its act of becoming is not extensive" (*Process and Reality*, page 69). Elsewhere: "A duration is a cross-section of the universe; it is the immediate present condition of the world at some epoch" (page 125). Elsewhere: "In the organic philosophy the notion of repetition is fundamental" (page 137). What else is *The Sonnets* but a portrait of becoming, consisting of durations that are cross-sections, and containing much repetition? It seems to have been his reading of Cage and Whitehead that made Ted sure of what he was doing, or going to do: *The Sonnets* feels deeper than its style and deeper than a "sonnet sequence" because of this underpinning. It is very seriously meant; and Ted never rejected in later life any of the thought behind the book. When he took up an idea, he scrutinized it closely and translated it into something his own and kept it: he was never fickle.

Ted's profound fidelity to his ideas is probably one reason why *The Sonnets* is so durable. Ted Berrigan isn't usually characterized as a deeply thoughtful poet, but that is probably because he tried so hard not to be boring and, within his capacity, to be ordinary. *The Sonnets* is not boring, being musical and sexy and funny and having the sound of ordinary people being named in various moods, though it is also fraught with the self-educational process, but that isn't necessarily an exotic or boring process either. Year after year *The Sonnets* continues to be both mysterious and manageable, but most especially it continues to be *there*: a "fact of modern poetry," as Frank O'Hara once said of it. It probably predicts subsequent works by other poets, and aspects of subsequent poetic movements, but that's not particularly important. What's important is that it's now timeless.

Thus we come to the subject of this new edition of *The Sonnets* and the reasons for it. The first two editions of *The Sonnets*, the "C" Press edition published in 1964, and the Grove Press edition published in 1967 (through the agency of Donald Allen), contained sixty-six of the original eighty-eight sonnets. In "Speaking of Picasso . . ." Ted says that "the ones that were cut were simply removed, and the Roman Numerals which serve as titles for most of the sonnets were not otherwise changed, so that the gaps became part of the sequence's construction." Further on, he adds, "I'd only been writing for a few years then . . . and only been living in New York for two and a half years, and I still believed the old line that one was supposed to ruthlessly cut everything until almost nothing was left." This is partly true, but all of the unincluded sonnets seem to have contained technical problems, many of which Ted gradually adjusted over the years. In 1982 United Artists published a new edition of *The Sonnets* including six previously unincluded ones: XXXIV, XXXV, LX, LXI, LXXVII, and LXXXI. Sonnets XXXIV and LXXXI had been published in *Red Wagon* in 1976.

In 1982, immediately after the publication of the United Artists edition, I showed Ted an original typescript of *The Sonnets*, including the rejected sonnets, which he'd given me some years previously and which he'd forgotten about. My typescript contained copies of unpublished sonnets he hadn't considered before because he'd been dealing with a different, incomplete typescript. He began tinkering again, and also annotating. As the result of a couple of days spent with my typescript in September of 1982, he decided that seven more sonnets were ready for inclusion: XIV, XXII, XXV, XXVIII, XXIX, XXXIII, LXIX. They are restored for the first time in the present edition. Ted's annotations, made ten months before his death, point toward a possible annotated edition at some time in the future, and are sketchy and uncompleted, but informative. They form the basis of my notes in the back. I've also sketchily identified Ted's friends, blues singers, certain kinds of names and references; in most cases, I have not identified established literary figures and artists or icons. The purpose of the notes is mainly to get down Ted's comments and to help elucidate his use of his friends' names, a literary device that is at least as old as Dante's work.

Finally, I would like to thank Doug Oliver, Ron Padgett, Anselm Berrigan, and Edmund Berrigan for their suggestions, advice, and legwork, and David Berrigan, Sarah Locke, and Jack and Sam Berrigan for general ambiance. And David Stanford for his continuous support.

Alice Notley
Paris, 1997, 2000

# THE SONNETS

*to Joe Brainard*

His piercing pince-nez. Some dim frieze
Hands point to a dim frieze, in the dark night.
In the book of his music the corners have straightened:
Which owe their presence to our sleeping hands.
The ox-blood from the hands which play
For fire for warmth for hands for growth
Is there room in the room that you room in?
Upon his structured tomb:
Still they mean something. For the dance
And the architecture.
Weave among incidents
May be portentous to him
We are the sleeping fragments of his sky,
Wind giving presence to fragments.

Dear Margie, hello. It is 5:15 a.m.
dear Berrigan. He died
Back to books. I read
It's 8:30 p.m. in New York and I've been running around all day
old come-all-ye's streel into the streets. Yes, it is now,
How Much Longer Shall I Be Able To Inhabit The Divine
and the day is bright gray turning green
feminine marvelous and tough
watching the sun come up over the Navy Yard
to write scotch-tape body in a notebook
had 17 and 1/2 milligrams
Dear Margie, hello. It is 5:15 a.m.
fucked til 7 now she's late to work and I'm
18 so why are my hands shaking I should know better

Stronger than alcohol, more great than song,
deep in whose reeds great elephants decay;
I, an island, sail, and my shores toss
on a fragrant evening, fraught with sadness
bristling hate.
It's true, I weep too much. Dawns break
slow kisses on the eyelids of the sea,
what other men sometimes have thought they've seen.
And since then I've been bathing in the poem
lifting her shadowy flowers up for me,
and hurled by hurricanes to a birdless place
the waving flags, nor pass by prison ships
O let me burst, and I be lost at sea!
and fall on my knees then, womanly.

IV

Lord, it is time. Summer was very great.
All sweetly spoke to her of me
about your feet, so delicate, and yet double E!!
And high upon the Brooklyn Bridge alone,
to breathe an old woman slop oatmeal,
loveliness that longs for butterfly! There is no pad
as you lope across the trails and bosky dells
I often think sweet and sour pork"
shoe repair, and scary. In cities,
I strain to gather my absurdities
He buckled on his gun, the one
Poised like Nijinsky
at every hand, my critic
and when I stand and clank it gives me shoes

Squawking a gala occasion, forgetting, and
"Hawkaaaaaaaaaa!" Once I went scouting
As stars are, like nightmares, a crucifix.
Why can't I read French? I don't know why can't you?
Rather the matter of growth
My babies parade waving their innocent flags
Huddled on the structured steps
Flinging currents into pouring streams
The "jeunes filles" so rare.
He wanted to know the *names*
He liked boys, never had a mother
Meanwhile, terrific misnomers went concocted, ayearning,
    ayearning
*The Pure No Nonsense*
And all day: Perceval! Perceval!

The bulbs burn phosphorescent, white
Your hair moves slightly,
Tenseness, but strength, outward
And the green rug nestled against the furnace
Dust had covered all the tacks, the hammer
. . . optimism for the jump . . .
The taste of such delicate thoughts
Never bring the dawn.
The bulbs burn, phosphorescent, white,
Melting the billowing snow with wine:
Could the mind turn jade? everything
Turning in this light, to stones,
Ash, bark like cork, a fading dust,
To cover the tracks of "The Hammer."

Whenever Richard Gallup is dissevered,
Fathers and teachers, and daemons down under the sea,
Audenesque Epithalamiums! She
Sends her driver home and she stays with me.

Match-Game etcetera! Bootleggers
Barrel-assing chevrolets grow bold. I summon
To myself sad silent thoughts,
Opulent, sinister, and cold.

Shall it be male or female in the tub?
And grawk go under, and grackle disappear,
And high upon the Brooklyn Bridge alone,
An ugly ogre masturbates by ear:

Of my darling, my darling, my pipe and my slippers,
Something there is is benzedrine in bed:
And so, so Asiatic, Richard Gallup
Goes home, and gets his gat, and plugs his dad.

She comes as in a dream with west wind eggs,
bringing Huitzilopochtli hot possets:
Snakeskins! But I am young, just old enough
to breathe, an old woman, slop oatmeal,
lemongrass, dewlarks, full draught of, fall thud.

Lady of the May, thou art fair,
Lady, thou art truly fair! Children,
When they see your face,
Sing in idiom of disgrace.

Pale like an ancient scarf, she is unadorned,
bouncing a red rubber ball in the veins.
The singer sleeps in Cos. Strange juxtaposed
the phantom sings: Bring me red demented rooms,
warm and delicate words! Swollen as if new-out-of-bed
Huitzilopochtli goes his dithyrambic way,
quick-shot, resuscitate, all roar!

My babies parade waving their innocent flags
an unpublished philosopher, a man who *must*
column after column down colonnade of rust
in my paintings, for they are present
I am wary of the mulctings of the pink promenade,
went in the other direction to Tulsa,
glistering, bristling, cozening whatever disguises
S of Christmas John Wayne will clown with
Dreams, aspirations of presence! Innocence gleaned,
annealed! The world in its mysteries are explained,
and the struggles of babies congeal. A hard core is formed.
"I wanted to be a cowboy." Doughboy will do.
Romance of it all was overwhelming
daylight of itself dissolving and of course it rained.

## 1. THE FOOL

He eats of the fruits of the great Speckle
Bird, pissing in the grass! Is it possible
He is incomplete, bringing you Ginger Ale
Of the interminably frolicsome gushing summer showers?
You were a Campfire Girl,
Only a part-time mother and father; I
Was large, stern, acrid, and undissuadable!
Ah, Bernie, we wear complete
The indexed Webster Unabridged Dictionary.
And lunch is not lacking, ants and clover
On the grass. To think of you alone
Suffering the poem of these states!
Oh Lord, it is bosky, giggling happy here,
And you, and me, the juice, at last extinct!

## 2. THE FIEND

Red-faced and romping in the wind
I too am reading the technical journals, but
Keeping Christmas-safe each city block
With tail-pin. My angels are losing patience,
Never win. Except at night. Then
I would like a silken thread
Tied round the solid blooming winter.
Trees stand stark-naked guarding bridal paths;
The cooling wind keeps blowing, and
There is a faint chance in geometric boxes!
It doesn't matter, though, to show he is
Your champion. Days are nursed on science fiction
And you tremble at the books upon the earth
As my strength and I walk out and look for you.

On the green a white boy goes
And he walks. Three ciphers and a faint fakir
No      One      Two      Three      Four      Today
I thought about all those radio waves
Winds flip down the dark path of breath
Passage      the treasure      Gomangani      I
Forget      bring the green boy white ways
And the wind goes there
Keats was a baiter of bears
Who died of lust      (You lie!      You lie!)
As so we all must in the green jungle
Under a sky of burnt umber we bumble to
The mien florist's to buy green nosegays
For the fey Saint's parade      Today
We may read about all those radio waves

Mountains of twine and
Teeth braced against it
Before gray walls. Feet walk
Released by night (which is not to imply
Death) under the murk spell
Racing down the blue lugubrious rainway
To the big promise of emptiness
In air we get our feet wet. . . . a big rock
Caresses cloud bellies
He finds he cannot fake
Wed to wakefulness, night which is not death
Fuscous with murderous dampness
But helpless, as blue roses are helpless.
Rivers of annoyance undermine the arrangements.

We remove a hand . . .
In a roomful of smoky man names burnished dull black
And labelled "blue" the din drifted in . . .
Someone said "Blake-blues" and someone else "pill-head"
Meaning bloodhounds. Someone shovelled in some
Cotton-field money brave free beer and finally "Negroes!"
They talked . . .
He thought of overshoes looked like mother
Made him
Combed his hair
Put away your hair. Books shall speak of us
When we are gone, like soft, dark scarves in gay April.
Let them discard loves in the Spring search! We
await a grass hand.

In Joe Brainard's collage its white arrow
He is not in it, the hungry dead doctor.
Of Marilyn Monroe, her white teeth white-
I am truly horribly upset because Marilyn
and ate King Korn popcorn," he wrote in his
of glass in Joe Brainard's collage
Doctor, but they say "I LOVE YOU"
and the sonnet is not dead.
takes the eyes away from the gray words,
*Diary.* The black heart beside the fifteen pieces
Monroe died, so I went to a matinee B-movie
washed by Joe's throbbing hands. "Today
What is in it is sixteen ripped pictures
does not point to William Carlos Williams.

# XVI

Into the closed air of the slow
Warmth comes, a slow going down of the Morning Land
She is warm. Into the vast closed air of the slow
Going down of the Morning Land
One vast under pinning trembles doom ice
Spreads beneath the mud troubled ice
Smother of a sword
Into her quick weak heat. She
Is introspection. One vast ice laden
Vast seas of doom and mud spread across the lake. Quick
  heat,
Of her vast ice laden self under introspective heat.
White lake trembles down to green goings
On, shades of a Chinese wall, itself "a signal."
It is a Chinese signal.

# XVII

*for Carol Clifford*

Each tree stands alone in stillness
After many years still nothing
The wind's wish is the tree's demand
The tree stands still
The wind walks up and down
Scanning the long selves of the shore
Her aimlessness is the pulse of the tree
It beats in tiny blots
Its patternless pattern of excitement
Letters     birds     beggars     books
There is no such thing as a breakdown
The tree     the ground     the wind     these are
Dear, be the tree your sleep awaits
Sensual, solid, still, swaying alone in the wind

Dear Marge, hello. It is 5:15 a.m.
Outside my room atonal sounds of rain
In my head. Dreams of Larry Walker
Drum in the pre-dawn. In my skull my brain
Season, cold images glitter brightly
In his marriage bed: of David Bearden
Answering. "Deteriorating," you said.
Say it. And made it hard to write. You know
Margie, tonight, and every night, in any
Aches in rhythm to that pounding morning rain.
Them over and over. And now I dread
Not a question, really, but you did
In your letter, many questions. I read
Paranoid: and of Martin Cochran, dead.

Harum-scarum haze on the Pollock streets
Where Snow White sleeps among the silent dwarfs
The fleet drifts in on an angry tidal wave
Or on the vast salt deserts of America
Drifts of Johann Strauss
A boy first sought in Tucson Arizona
The withering weathers of
Melodic signs of Arabic adventure
Of polytonic breezes gathering in the gathering winds
Mysterious Billy Smith a fantastic trigger
Of a plush palace shimmering velvet red
The cherrywood romances of rainy cobblestones
A dark trance
In the trembling afternoon

On the green a white boy goes
We may read about all those radio waves
And he walks. Three ciphers and a faint fakir
For the fey Saint's parade      Today
No      One      Two      Three      Four      Today
Under a sky of burnt umber we bumble to
Forget      Bring the green boy white ways
As so we all must in the green jungle
Winds flip down the dark path of breath
The mien florist's to buy green nosegays
Passage      the treasure      Gomangani
I thought about all those radio waves
Keats was a baiter of bears
Who died of lust   (You lie!    You lie!)
And the wind goes there

## XXII

Go fly a kite he writes
Who cannot escape his own blue hair
who storms to the big earth and is not absent-minded
& Who dumbly begs a key      & who cannot pay his way
Racing down the blue lugubrious rainway
day brakes and night is a quick pick-me-up
Rain is a wet high harried face
To walk is wet hurried high safe and game
Tiny bugs flit from pool to field and light on every bulb
Whose backs hide doors down round wind-tunnels
He is an umbrella. . . .
Many things are current
Simple night houses rain
Standing pat in the breathless blue air.

# XXIII

On the 15th day of November in the year of the motorcar
Between Oologah and Pawnee
A hand is writing these lines
In a roomful of smoky man names burnished dull black
Southwest, lost doubloons rest, no comforts drift
On dream smoke down the sooted fog ravine
In a terrible Ozark storm the Tundra vine
Blood ran like muddy inspiration: Walks he in around anyway
The slight film has gone to gray-green children
And seeming wide night. Now night
Is a big drink of waterbugs      Then were we so fragile
Honey scorched our lips
On the 15th day of November in the year of the motorcar
Between Oologah and Pawnee

Mud on the first day (night, rather
I was thinking of Bernard Shaw, of sweet May Morris
Do you want me to take off my dress?
Some Poems!
the aeroplane waiting to take you on your first
getting used to using each other
Cowboys!      and banging on my sorrow, with books
*The Asiatics*
believed in tree spirits, a tall oak, swans gone in the rain,
a postcard of Juan Gris      not a word
Fell on the floor      how strange      to be gone in a minute
I came to you by bus      to be special for us
The bellboy      letters      a key      then to hear from an old stranger
The Gift:      they will reside in Houston following the Grand Canyon.

# XXVI

*One Sonnet for Dick*

This excitement to be all of night, Henry!
Elvis Peering-Eye danced with Carol Clifford, high,
Contrived whose leaping herb edifies Kant! I'll bust!
Smile! "Got rye in this'n?"
Widow Dan sold an eye t'meander an X. Whee! Yum!
Pedant tore her bed! Tune, hot! Full cat saith why foo?
"Tune hot full cat?" "No! nexus neck ink!
All moron (on) while "weighed in fur" pal! "Ah'm Sun!"
Dayday came to get her daddy. "Daddy,"
Saith I to Dick in the verge, (In the Verge!)
And "gee" say I, "Easter" "fur" "few tears" "Dick!"
My Carol now a Museum! "O, Ma done fart!" "Less full
Cat," she said, "One's there!" "Now cheese, ey?"
"Full cat wilted, bought ya a pup!" "So, nose excitement?"

Andy Butt was drunk in the Parthenon
Bar. If only the Greeks were a band-
Aid, he thought. Then my woe would not flow
O'er the land. He considered his honeydew
Hand. "O woe, woe!" saith Andrew, "a fruit
In my hand may suffice to convey me to Greece,
But I must have envy to live! A grasshopper,
George, if you please!" The bartender sees
That our Andrew's awash on the sofa
Of wide melancholy. His wound he refurbishes
Stealthily shifty-eyed over the runes. "Your
Trolleycar, sir," 's said to Andy, "you bloody
Well emptied the Parthenon!" "A fruitful vista
This Our South," laughs Andrew to his Pa,
But his rough woe slithers o'er the Land.

to gentle, pleasant strains
just homely enough
to be beautiful
in the dark neighborhoods of my own sad youth
i fall in love.   once
seven thousand feet over one green schoolboy summer
i dug two hundred graves,
laughing, "Put away your books! Who shall speak of us
when we are gone? Let them wear scarves
in the once a day snow, crying in the kitchen
of my heart!" O my love, I will weep a less bitter truth,
till other times, making a minor repair,
a breath of cool rain in those streets
clinging together with slightly detached air.

Now she guards her chalice in a temple of fear
Calm before a storm. Yet your brooding eyes
Or acquiescence soon cease to be answers.
And your soft, dark hair, a means of speaking
Becomes too much to bear. Sometimes,
In a rare, unconscious moment,
Alone this sudden darkness in a toybox
Christine's classic beauty, Okinawa
To Laugh (Autumn gone, and Spring a long way
Off)     is loving you
When need exceeds means,
I read the Evening World / the sports,
The funnies, the vital statistics, the news:
Okinawa was a John Wayne movie to me.

# XXX

Into the closed air of the slow
Now she guards her chalice in a temple of fear
Each tree stands alone in stillness
to gentle, pleasant strains
Dear Marge, hello. It is 5:15 a.m.
Andy Butt was drunk in the Parthenon
Harum-scarum haze on the Pollock streets
This excitement to be all of night, Henry!
Ah, Bernie, to think of you alone, suffering
It is such a good thing to be in love with you
On the green a white boy goes
He's braver than I, brother
Many things are current, and of these the least are
    not always children
On the 15th day of November in the year of the motorcar

# XXXI

And then one morning to waken perfect-faced
To the big promise of emptiness
In a terrible Ozark storm
Pleasing John Greenleaf Whittier!
Speckled marble bangs against his soiled green feet
And each sleeping son is broke-backed and dumb
In fever and sleep processional
Voyages harass the graver
And grope underneath the most serious labor
Darius feared the boats. Meanwhile
John Greenleaf Whittier was writing. Meanwhile
Grandma thought wistfully of international sock fame
Down the John G. Whittier Railroad Road
In the morning sea mouth

# XXXII

The blue day! In the air winds dance
Now our own children are strangled down in the bubbling
    quadrangle.
To thicken! He felt his head
Returning past the houses he passed
"Goodbye, Bernie!"     "Goodbye, Carol!"     "Goodbye,
    Marge!"
Davy Crockett was nothing like Jesse James
A farmer drove up on a tractor
He said he was puzzled by the meaning exactly of "block".
The blue day! Where else can we go
To escape from our tedious homes, and perhaps recapture
    the past?
Now our own children are returning past the houses
I sit at my dust-patterned desk littered with four month
    dust
The air beginning to thicken
In the square, on the farm, in my white block hair

Où sont les neiges des neiges?
The most elegant present I could get.
The older children weep among the flowers.
They believe this. Their laughter feeds the need
Like a juggler. Ten weeks pregnant. Who
Believes this? It is your love
Must feed the dancing snow, Mary
Shelley "created" Frankenstein. It doesn't
matter, though. The shortage of available materials
Shatters my zest with festivity, one
Trembling afternoon—night—the dark trance
Up rainy cobblestones     bottle half empty
Full throttle     mired
In the petty frustrations of off-white sheets

# XXXIV

Time flies by like a great whale
And I find my hand grows stale at the throttle
Of my many faceted and fake appearance
Who bucks and spouts by detour under the sheets
Hollow portals of solid appearance
Movies are poems, a holy bible, the great mother to us
People go by in the fragrant day
Accelerate softly my blood
But blood is still blood and tall as a mountain blood
Behind me green rubber grows, feet walk
In wet water, and dusty heads grow wide
Padré, Father, or fat old man, as you will,
I am afraid to succeed, afraid to fail
Tell me now, again, who I am

# XXXV

You can make this swooped transition on your lips
Go to the sea, the lake, the tree
And the dog days come
Your head spins when the old bull rushes
Back in the airy daylight, he was not a midget
And preferred to be known as a stunt-man.
His stand-in was named Herman, but came rarely.
Why do you begin to yawn so soon, who seemed
So hard, feather-bitten     back in the airy daylight
Put away your hair. The black heart beside the 15 pieces
    of glass
Spins when the old bull rushes. The words say I LOVE YOU
Go to the sea, the lake, the tree
Glistering, bristling, cozening whatever disguises

# XXXVI

*after Frank O'Hara*

It's 8:54 a.m. in Brooklyn it's the 28th of July and
it's probably 8:54 in Manhattan but I'm
in Brooklyn I'm eating English muffins and drinking
pepsi and I'm thinking of how Brooklyn is New
York city too how odd I usually think of it as
something all its own like Bellows Falls like Little
Chute like Uijongbu
                  I never thought on the Williams-
burg bridge I'd come so much to Brooklyn
just to see lawyers and cops who don't even carry
guns taking my wife away and bringing her back
                                  No
and I never thought Dick would be back at Gude's
beard shaved off long hair cut and Carol reading
his books when we were playing cribbage and
watching the sun come up over the Navy Yard
across the river
                  I think I was thinking when I was
ahead I'd be somewhere like Perry street erudite
dazzling slim and badly loved
contemplating my new book of poems
to be printed in simple type on old brown paper
feminine marvelous and tough

# XXXVII

It is night. You are asleep. And beautiful tears
Have blossomed in my eyes. Guillaume Apollinaire is dead.
The big green day today is singing to itself
A vast orange library of dreams, dreams
Dressed in newspaper, wan as pale thighs
Making vast apple strides towards "The Poems."
"The Poems" is not a dream. It is night. You
Are asleep. Vast orange libraries of dreams
Stir inside "The Poems." On the dirt-covered ground
Crystal tears drench the ground. Vast orange dreams
Are unclenched. It is night. Songs have blossomed
In the pale crystal library of tears. You
Are asleep. A lovely light is singing to itself,
In "The Poems," in my eyes, in the line, "Guillaume
    Apollinaire is dead."

Sleep half sleep half silence and with reasons
For you I starred in the movie
Made on the site
Of Benedict Arnold's triumph, Ticonderoga, and
I shall increase from this
As I am a cowboy and you imaginary
Ripeness begins corrupting every tree
Each strong morning      A man signs a shovel
And so he digs      It hurts      and so
We get our feet wet in air      we love our lineage
Ourselves      Music, salve, pills, kleenex, lunch
And the promise never to truckle      A man
Breaks his arm and so he sleeps      he digs
In sleep half silence and with reason

# MESS OCCUPATIONS

*after Michaux*

A few rape men or kill coons so I bat them!
Daughter prefers to lay 'em on a log and tear their hair.
    Moaning Jimmy bats her!
"Ill yeah!" da junky says. "I aint as fast no more,
    I'll rent a lot in a cemetree."    He'll recite it
    two times scary sunday O sea-daisy o'er a shade!
Au revoir, scene!
She had a great toe!
She-tail's raggy, too!
Jelly bend over put'im on too!
She laid a crab!
Jelly him sure later! Jelly-ass ails are tough!
She lays all his jelly on him!
Eeeeeeooooowww!! La Vie!
Her lay races is out here, she comes on, I'm on her, I'll
fart in one ear! "Jelly, sir?" "Shall I raise him yet?"
Long-toed we dance on where Shit-toe can see ten blue men
lickin' ten new partners and the sucker's son!
"Mating, Madame, can whip you up up!
My Jimmy's so small he wiggles plum moans! Ladies shimmy
at Jimmy in waves

# XL

Wan as pale thighs making apple belly strides
In the morning she wakes up, and she is "in love."
One red finger sports a gold finger-gripper
Curled to honor *La Pluie*, by Max Jacob. Max Jacob,
When I lie down to love you, I am one hundred times more
A ghost! My dreams of love have haunted you for years
More than six-pointed key olive shame. Not this day
Shall my pale apple dreams know my dream "English
    muffins, broken arm"
Nor my dream where the George Gordon gauge reads, "a
Syntactical error, Try Again!" Gosh, I gulp to be here
In my skin, writing, *The Dwarf of Ticonderoga*. Icy girls
finger thighs bellies apples in my dream the big gunfire
    sequence
For the Jay Kenneth Koch movie, *Phooey!* I recall
My Aunt Annie and begin.

banging around in a cigarette      she isn't "in love"
my dream a drink with Ira Hayes we discuss the code of
   the west
my hands make love to my body when my arms are around you
you never tell me your name
and I am forced to write "belly" when I mean "love"
Au revoir, scene!
I waken, read, write long letters and
wander restlessly when leaves are blowing
my dream a crumpled horn
in advance of the broken arm
she murmurs of signs to her fingers
weeps in the morning to waken so shackled with love
Not me. I like to beat people up.
My dream a white tree

She murmurs of signs to her fingers
Not this day
Breaks his arm and so he sleeps      he digs
Dressed in newspaper, wan as pale thighs
beard shaved off long hair cut and Carol reading
Put away your hair. The black heart beside the 15 pieces
     of glass
Of my many faceted and fake appearance
The most elegant present I could get!
"Goodbye, Bernie!"      "Goodbye, Carol!"      "Goodbye,
     Marge!"
Speckled marble bangs against his soiled green feet
And seeming wide night. Now night
Where Snow White sleeps amongst the silent dwarfs
Drifts of Johann Strauss
It is 5:15 a.m.      Dear Marge, hello.

in my paintings for they are present
Dreams, aspirations of presence! And he walks
Wed to wakefulness, night which is not death
Rivers of annoyance undermine the arrangements
We remove a hand . . .
washed by Joe's throbbing hands. "Today
itself "a signal." She
is introspection.
Each tree stands alone in stillness
Scanning the long selves of the shore.
In Joe Brainard's collage, there is no such thing
as a breakdown.
Trains go by, and they *are* trains. He hears the feet of the men
Racing to beg him to wait

The withered leaves fly higher than dolls can see
A watchdog barks in the night
Joyful ants nest in the roof of my tree
There is only off-white mescalin to be had
Anne is writing poems to me and worrying about "making it"
and Ron is writing poems and worrying about "making it"
and Pat is worrying but not working on anything
and Gude is worrying about his sex life
It is 1959, and I am waiting for the mail
Who cares about Tuesday (Jacques Louis David normalcy day)?
Boston beat New York three to one. It could have been
Carolyn. Providence is as close to Montana as Tulsa.
He buckles on his gun, the one Steve left him:
His stand-in was named Herman, but came rarely

What thwarts this fear I love
to hear it creak upon this shore
of the trackless room;      the sea, night, lilacs
all getting ambiguous
Who dreams on the black colonnade
Casually tossed off as well
Are dead after all (and who falters?)
Everything turns into writing
I strain to gather my absurdities into a symbol
Every day my bridge
They basted his caption on top of the fat sheriff, "The Pig."
Some "others" were dormants: More water went under the dam.
What excitement to think of her returning, over the colonnade,
over the tall steppes, warm hands guiding his eyes to hers

## LINES FOR LAUREN OWEN

Harum-scarum haze on the Pollock streets
The fleet drifts in on an angry tidal wave
Drifts of Johann Strauss
The withering weather of
Of polytonic breezes gathering in the gathering winds
Of a plush palace shimmering velvet red
In the trembling afternoon
A dark trance
The cherrywood romances of rainy cobblestones
Mysterious Billy Smith a fantastic trigger
Melodic signs of Arabic adventure
A boy first sought in Tucson Arizona
Or on the vast salt deserts of America
Where Snow White sleeps among the silent dwarfs

gray his head goes        his feet green
No lady dream around in any bad exposure
"no pipe dream, sir. She would be the dragon
Head, dapple green of mien. must be vacated
in favor of double-clutching, and sleep,
seldom, though deep. We savor its sodden dungheap flavor
on our creep toward the rational. William Bonney
buried his daddy and killed a many. Benito Mussolini
proved a defective, but Ezra Pound came down, came
down and went. And so, Carol, remember,
We are each free to shed big crystal tears on
The dirt-covered ground, tied together only
By white clouds and some mud we can find, if we try,
In the darksome orange shadows of the big blue swamp

Francis Marion nudges himself gently into the big blue sky
The farm was his family farm
On the real farm
                    I understood "The Poems."
The dust fissure drains the gay dance
Home returning on the blue winds of dust.
A farmer rides a tractor. It is a block
To swallow. Thus a man lives by his tooth.
Meaning strides through these poems just as it strides
Through me! When I traipse on my spunk, I get
Wan! Traipse on my spunk and I get wan, too!
    Francis Marion
Muscles down in tooth-clenched strides toward
The effort regulator: His piercing pince-nez
Some dim frieze in "The Poems" and these go on without me

Joyful ants nest on the roof of my tree
Crystal tears wed to wakefulness
My dream a crumpled horn
Ripeness begins in advance of the broken arm
The black heart two times scary Sunday
Pale thighs making apple belly strides
And he walks. Beside the fifteen pieces of glass
A postcard of Juan Gris
Vast orange dreams wed to wakefulness
Swans gone in the rain came down, came down and went
Warm hands corrupting every tree
Guiding his eyes to her or a shade
Ripeness begins     My dream a crumpled horn
Fifteen pieces of glass on the roof of my tree

I like to beat people up
absence of passion, principles, love. She murmurs
What just popped into my eye was a fiend's umbrella
and if you should come and pinch me now
as I go out for coffee
. . . as I was saying winter of 18 lumps
Days produce life locations to banish 7 up
Nomads, my babies, where are you? Life's
My dream which is gunfire in my poem
Orange cavities of dreams stir inside "The Poems"
Whatever is going to happen is already happening
Some people prefer "the interior monologue"
I like to beat people up

Summer so histrionic, marvelous dirty days
is not genuine     it shines forth from the faces
littered with soup, cigarette butts, the heavy
is a correspondent     the innocence of childhood
sadness graying the faces of virgins aching
and everything comes before their eyes
to be fucked, we fondle their snatches but they
that the angels have supereminent wisdom is shown
they weep and get solemn etcetera
from thought     for all things come to them gratuitously
by their speech     it flows directly and spontaneously
and O I am afraid! but later they'll be eyeing the butts of
    the studs
in the street rain flushing the gutters bringing from Memphis
Gus Cannon gulping, "I called myself Banjo Joe!"

# LII

*for Richard White*

It is a human universe: & I
is a correspondent      The innocence of childhood
is not genuine      it shines forth from the faces
The poem upon the page is as massive as Anne's thighs
Belly to hot belly we have laid

                              baffling combustions
are everywhere      graying the faces of virgins
aching to be fucked      we fondle their snatches
and O, I am afraid!      The poem upon the page
will not kneel      for everything comes to it
gratuitously      like Gertrude Stein to Radcliffe
Gus Cannon to say "I called myself Banjo Joe!"
O wet kisses, death on earth, lovely fucking in the poem
   upon the page,
you have kept up with the times, and I am glad!

The poem upon the page is as massive as
Anne's thighs      belly to hot belly we have laid
Serene beneath feverous folds, flashed cool
in our white heat      hungered      and tasted      and
Gone to the movies      baffling combustions
are everywhere!      like Gertrude Stein at Radcliffe,
Patsy Padgett replete with teen-age belly!      every-
one's suddenly pregnant and no one is glad!
O wet kisses, the poem upon the page
Can tell you about teeth you've never dreamed
Could bite, nor be such reassurance! Babies are not
Like Word Origins and cribbage boards      or dreams
of correspondence!      Fucking is so very lovely
Who can say no to it later?

# LV

Grace to be born and live as variously as possible
White boats     green banks     black dust     atremble
Massive as Anne's thighs upon the page
I rage in a blue shirt at a brown desk in a
Bright room sustained by a bellyful of pills
"The Poems" is not a dream     for all things come to them
Gratuitously     In quick New York we imagine the blue Charles
Patsy awakens in heat and ready to squabble
No Poems she demands in a blanket command     belly
To hot belly we have laid     serenely white
Only my sweating pores are true in the empty night
Baffling combustions are everywhere!     we hunger and taste
And go to the movies     then run home drenched in flame
To the grace of the make-believe bed

banging around in a cigarette     she isn't "in love"
She murmurs of signs to her fingers
in my paintings for they are present
The withered leaves fly higher than dolls can see
What thwarts this fear I love
Mud on the first day (night, rather
gray his head goes     his feet green
Francis Marion nudges himself gently in the big blue sky
Joyful ants nest on the roof of my tree
I like to beat people up.
Summer so histrionic, marvelous dirty days
It is a human universe: & I
sings like Casals in furtive dark July; Out we go
to the looney movie     to the make-believe bed

Patsy awakens in heat and ready to squabble
In a bright room sustained by a bellyful of pills
One's suddenly pregnant and no one is glad!
Aching to be fucked we fondle their snatches
That the angels have supereminent wisdom is shown
Days produce life locations to banish 7 Up
A postcard of Juan Gris
To swallow. Thus a man lives by his tooth.
Buried his daddy and killed a many. Benito Mussolini
*The Asiatics*
Everything turns into writing
And Gude is worrying about his sex life
Each tree is introspection
The most elegant present I could get

In Joe Brainard's collage its white arrow
does not point to William Carlos Williams.
He is not in it, the hungry dead doctor.
What is in it is sixteen ripped pictures
Of Marilyn Monroe, her white teeth white-
washed by Joe's throbbing hands. "Today
I am truly horribly upset because Marilyn
Monroe died, so I went to a matinee B-movie
and ate King Korn popcorn," he wrote in his
*Diary*. The black heart beside the fifteen pieces
of glass in Joe Brainard's collage
takes the eye away from the gray words,
Doctor, but they say "I LOVE YOU"
and the sonnet is not dead.

old prophets    Help me to believe
New York!    sacerdotal    drink it take a pill
Blocks of blooming winter.    Patricia was a
bed    Patsy    gone    The best fighter in Troy
Be bride and groom and priest:    in pajamas
Sweet girls will bring you candied apples!
Drummer-boys and Choo-Choos will astound you!
Areté    I    thus I    Again I    I
An Organ-Grinder's monkey does his dance.
Ted    Ron    Dick    Didactic    un-melodic
Roisterers here assembled shatter my zest
Berrigan    secretly    HEKTOR    GAME ETC.
More books!    Rilke    Stevens    Pound    Auden
    & Frank
Some kind of Bowery Santa Clauses    I wonder
Who am about to die    the necessary lies

# LXI

How sweet the downward sweep of your prickly thighs
as you lope across the trails and bosky dells
defying natural law, saying, "Go Fuck Yourselves,
You Motherfuckers!" You return me to Big Bill Broonzy
and Guillaume Apollinaire and when you devour your young,
the natural philosophy of love,
I am moved as only I am moved by the singing of the
    Stabat Mater at Sunday Mass.
How succulent your flesh sometimes so tired
from losing its daily battles with its dead! All
this and the thought that you go to the bathroom
fills me with love for you, makes me love you even more
    than the dirt
in the crevices in my window
and the rust on the bolt in my door
in terms I contrived as a boy, such as
"making it"      "fuck them"      and
"I know you have something to tell me."

Is there room in the room that you room in?
fucked til 7 now she's late to work and I'm
18 so why are my hands shaking I should know better
Stronger than alcohol, more great than song
O let me burst, and I be lost at sea!
and I fall on my knees then, womanly.
to breathe an old woman slop oatmeal
Why can't I read French? I don't know why can't you?
The taste of such delicate thoughts
Never bring the dawn.
                              To cover the tracks
of "The Hammer."
Something there is is benzedrine in bed:
                              Bring me red demented rooms,
warm and delicate words

# LXV

Dreams, aspirations of presence! Innocence gleaned,
annealed! The world in its mysteries are explained,
and the struggles of babies congeal. A hard core is formed.
Today I thought about all those radio waves
He eats of the fruits of the great Speckle bird,
Pissing on the grass!
I too am reading the technical journals,
Rivers of annoyance undermine the arrangements
Someone said "Blake-blues" and someone else "pill-head"
Meaning bloodhounds.
Washed by Joe's throbbing hands
She is introspection.
It is a Chinese signal.
There is no such thing as a breakdown

# LXVI

it was summer. We were there. And THERE WAS NO
MONEY.                                   you are like . . .
skyscrapers veering away
a B-29 plunging to Ploesti
sailboat scudding thru quivering seas
trembling velvet red in the shimmering afternoon
     darkness of sea
     The sea which is cool and green
     The sea which is dark, cool, and green
I am closing my window. Tears silence the wind.
"they'll pick us off like sittin' ducks"
Sundown. Manifesto. Color and cognizance.
Then to cleave to a cast-off emotion,
(clarity! clarity!) a semblance of motion, omniscience

(clarity! clarity!) a semblance of motion, omniscience.
There is no such thing as a breakdown
To cover the tracks of "The Hammer"     (the morning sky
gets blue and red and I get worried about
mountains of mounting pressure
and the rust on the bolt in my door
Some kind of Bowery Santa Clauses        I wonder
down the secret streets of Roaring Gap
A glass of chocolate milk, head of lettuce, dark-
Bearden is dead. Chris is dead. Jacques Villon is dead.
Patsy awakens in heat and ready to squabble
I wonder if people talk about me *secretly?* I wonder if I'm
    fooling myself
about pills? I wonder what's in the icebox? out we go
to the looney movie     and the grace of the make-believe bed

I am closing my window. Tears silence the wind.
and the rust on the bolt in my door
Mud on the first day (night, rather
littered with soup, cigarette butts, the heavy
getting used to using each other
my dream a drink with Ira Hayes we discuss the code of the west
I think I was thinking when I was ahead
To the big promise of emptiness
This excitement to be all of night, Henry!
Three ciphers and a faint fakir. And he walks.
White lake trembles down to green goings on
Of the interminably frolicsome gushing summer showers
Everything turning in this light to stones
Which owe their presence to our sleeping hands

# LXX

*after Arthur Rimbaud*

Sweeter than sour apples flesh to boys
The brine of brackish water pierced my hulk
Cleansing me of rot-gut wine and puke
Sweeping away my anchor in its swell
And since then I've been bathing in the poem
Of the star-steeped milky flowing mystic sea
Devouring great sweeps of azure green and
Watching flotsam, dead men, float by me
Where, dyeing all the blue, the maddened flames
And stately rhythms of the sun, stronger
Than alcohol, more great than song,
Fermented the bright red bitterness of love
I've seen skies split with light, and night,
And surfs, currents, waterspouts; I know
What evening means, and doves, and I have seen
What other men sometimes have thought they've seen

"I know what evening means, and doves, and I have seen
What other men sometimes have thought they've seen:"
(to cleave to a cast-off emotion—Clarity! Clarity!)
my dream a drink with Richard Gallup we discuss the code
of the west      of the interminably frolicsome
gushing summer showers      getting used to "I am closing
my window."      my dream a drink with Henry Miller
too soon for the broken arm.      Hands point to a dim frieze
in the dark night.      Wind giving presence to fragments.
Shall it be male or female in the tub?
Barrel-assing chevrolets grow bold. I summon to myself
"The Asiatic"   (and grawk go under, and grackle disappear,)
Sundown. Manifesto. Color and cognizance.
And to cleave to a semblance of motion. Omniscience

# LXXII

## A SONNET FOR DICK GALLUP
### / July 1963

The logic of grammar is not genuine      it shines forth
From The Boats      We fondle the snatches of virgins
     aching to be fucked
And O, I am afraid!      Our love has red in it      and
I become finicky as in an abstraction!
                                             (. . . but lately
I'm always lethargic . . .      the last heavy sweetness
through the wine . . .)
                         Who dwells alone
                         Except at night
(. . . basted the shackles the temporal music the spit)
     Southwest lost doubloons rest, no comforts drift on
dream smoke
                    (my dream      the big earth)
On the green a white boy goes      to not
Forget      Released by night (which is not to imply
Clarity      The logic is not The Boats      and O, I am not alone

Dear Ron:      Keats was a baiter of bears      etc.
Tenseness, but strength, outward      And the green
flinging currents into pouring streams      The "Jeunes filles"
so rare      Today I think about all those radio waves
a slow going down of the Morning Land
the great Speckle bird at last extinct      (a reference
to Herman Melville)      at heart we are infinite, we are
ethereal, we are weird!      Each tree stands alone in stillness.
Your head spins when the old bull rushes      (Back in the city
He was not a midget, and preferred to be known as a stuntman)
Gosh, I gulp to be here in my skin! What thwarts this fear
I love      Everything turns into writing (and who falters)
I LIKE TO BEAT PEOPLE UP!!!      (absence of principles,
    passion
) love.      White boats   Green banks      Grace to be born and
    live

# LXXIV

"*The academy*
*of the future*
*is opening its doors*"
—JOHN ASHBERY

The academy of the future is opening its doors
my dream a crumpled horn
Under the blue sky the big earth is floating into "The Poems."
"A fruitful vista, this, our South," laughs Andrew to his Pa.
But his rough woe slithers o'er the land.
Ford Madox Ford is not a dream. The farm
was the family farm. On the real farm
I understood "The Poems."
                    Red-faced and romping in the wind, I, too,
am reading the technical journals. The only travelled sea
that I still dream of
is a cold black pond, where once
on a fragrant evening fraught with sadness
I launched a boat frail as a butterfly

Seurat and Juan Gris combine this season
to outline Central Park in geometric
trillion pointed bright red-brown and green-gold
blocks of blooming winter. Trees stand stark-
naked guarding bridal paths like Bowery
Santa Clauses keeping Christmas safe each city block.
Thus I, red faced and romping in the wind
Whirl thru mad Manhattan dressed in books
looking for today with tail-pin. I
never place it right, never win. It
doesn't matter, though. The cooling wind keeps blow-
ing and my poems are coming.
Except at night. Then
I walk out in the bleak village and look for you

# LXXVI

I wake up back aching from soft bed Pat
gone to work Ron to class (I
never heard a sound) it's my birthday. I put on
birthday pants birthday shirt go to ADAM's buy a
pepsi for breakfast come home drink it take a pill
I'm high. I do three Greek lessons
to make up for cutting class. I read birthday book
(from Joe) on Juan Gris real name José Vittoriano
Gonzáles stop in the middle read all
my poems gloat a little over new ballad quickly skip old
sonnets imitations of Shakespeare. Back to books. I read
poems by Auden Spenser Pound Stevens and Frank O'Hara.
     I hate books.
          I wonder if Jan or Helen or Babe
ever think about me. I wonder if Dave Bearden still
dislikes me. I wonder if people talk about me
secretly. I wonder if I'm too old. I wonder if I'm fooling
myself about pills. I wonder what's in the icebox. I wonder
if Ron or Pat bought any toilet paper this morning

"DEAR CHRIS

it is 3:17 a.m. in New York city, yes, it is
1962, it is the year of parrot fever. In
Brandenburg, and by the granite gates, the
old come-all-ye's streel into the streets. Yes, it is now,
the season of delight. I am writing to you to say that
I have gone mad. Now I am sowing the seeds which shall,
when ripe, master the day, and
portion out the night. Be watching for me when blood
flows down the streets. Pineapples are a sign
that I am coming. My darling, it is nearly time. Dress
the snowman in the Easter sonnet we made for him
when scissors were in style. For now, goodbye, and
all my love,
          The Snake."

Too many fucking mosquitoes under the blazing sun
out in the stinking alley behind my desk!      too many
lovely delicious behinds fertilizing the park! the logic
of childhood is not genuine      it shines forth
so rare
            Dear Ron: Keats was a baiter of bears who died
of lust! Today I think about all those radio waves
The academy of my dreams is opening its doors
Seurat and Juan Gris combine this season
Except at night!
                        Then I walk out in the bleak village
in my dreams, for they are present! I wake up
aching from soft bed      Back to books. It is 3:17 a.m. in
   New York city
*The Pure No Nonsense:* and all day "Perceval! Perceval!"

# LXXX

How strange to be gone in a minute
Bearden is dead     Gallup is dead     Margie is dead
Patsy awakens in heat and ready to squabble
Dear Chris, hello. It is 5:15 a.m.
I rage in a blue shirt, at a brown desk, in
A bright room, sustained by the darkness outside and
A cast-off emotion. A hard core is "formed"
That the angels have supereminent wisdom is shown
"He Shot Me" was once my favorite poem
Speckled marble makes my eyes ache as I rest on
The only major statement in New York city     Louis Sullivan
is dead     whose grief I would most assuage
"He Shot Me" is still my favorite poem, and
"I Don't See Any Anchor Tied To Your Ass"

Musick strides through these poems
just as it strides through me! The red block
Dream of Hans Hoffman keeps going away and
Coming back to me. He is not "The Poems."
        (my dream a drink with Lonnie Johnson we
discuss the code of the west)
                      How strange to be gone
                      in a minute!
too soon for the broken arm. Ripeness begins corrupting every
   tree
Each strong morning      in air we get our feet wet
                           (my dream
a crumpled horn)     it hurts.     Huddie Ledbetter is dead
whose griefs I would most assuage     Sing I must     And
   with Musick I must rage
Against those whose griefs I would most assuage
       (my dream
"DEAR CHRIS, hello. It is 3:17 a.m.

my dream a drink with Lonnie Johnson we discuss the code
   of the west
The red block dream of Hans Hofmann keeps going away
   and coming back to me
my dream a crumpled horn
my dream DEAR CHRIS, hello. It is 5:15 a.m.
The academy of my dreams is opening its doors
Ford Madox Ford is not a dream.
The only travelled sea that I still dream of is a cold black pond
   where once on a fragrant evening fraught with sadness
   I launched a boat frail as a butterfly
Southwest lost doubloons rest, no comforts drift on dream
   smoke down the sooted fog ravine
My dream a drink with Richard Gallup we discuss the code
   of the west
my dream a drink with Henry Miller
"The Poems" is not a dream.
Vast orange dreams wed to wakefulness: icy girls finger thighs
   bellies apples in my dream the big gunfire sequence for
   the Jay Kenneth Koch movie, *Phooey!*
My dream a drink with Ira Hayes we discuss the code of the west

Woman is singing the song and summer
Only to others, meaning poems. Because everything
Sorry about West Point. But where else was one to go,
Southwest lost doubloons rest, no comforts drift on dream smoke
Against whose griefs I would most assuage
(A cast-off emotion) A hard core is "formed."
Musick strides through these poems just as it strides thru me
my dream a drink with Lonnie Johnson we discuss the code
    of the west
After Ticonderoga.      Beware of Benjamin Franklin, he is
    totally lacking in grace
What else. Because he tended to think of truth as "The King's
    Birthday List"
This is called "Black Nausea" by seers.
My dream DEAR CHRIS hello. It is 3:17 a.m.
Your name is now a household name, as is mine. And in any case,
although I failed, now we need never be rivals

LXXXIV

Dear Ron: hello. Your name is now a household name,
As is mine. We, too, suffer black spells. This is called
"Black Nausea" by seers, only to others, meaning poems.
In every way now we are equal. Except one.
Ford Madox Ford is not a dream.      (my dream a drink
with Henry Miller) we discuss the code of the west.
He is not "The Poems."
                          "He Shot Me" was once my favorite
Cast-off emotion. Now I rage in a blue shirt at a brown desk
In a bright room. In Tulsa Chris has said goodbye to Bernie.
I never beat people up. The academy of my dreams
is opening its doors / a fat black woman is singing a song and
Summer is the subject matter. Next to her his nose couldn't grow
Even if it does choke you up, and these marvelous tears
   keep appearing

They basted his caption on top of the fat sheriff, "The Pig."
Cowboys       and banging on my sorrow with books
No lady dream around in any bad exposure
The dust fissure drains the gay dance
Joyful ants nest in the roof of my tree
absence of passion, principles, love. She murmurs
is not genuine. it shines forth from the faces
And each sleeping son is broke-backed and dumb.
Davy Crockett was nothing like Jesse James
The most elegant present I could get!
But blood is still blood and tall as a mountain blood
Go to the sea, the lake, the tree
dazzling slim and badly loved
You are asleep. A lovely light is singing to itself

# LXXXVII

Beware of Benjamin Franklin, he is totally lacking in grace
This is called "Black Nausea" by seers. (They basted his caption
on top of the fat sheriff)
                              These sonnets are a homage to
King Ubu.
Fasten your crimson garter around his servile heart
With which he pours forth interminably
The poem of these states      scanning the long selves of
the shore      and      "gift gift"
Great black rat packs were running amuck amidst the murk
of these states      Outside my room
These sonnets are a homage to myself
absence of passion, principles, love
The most elegant present I could get!      (This is called
"Black Nausea" by seers)

# LXXXVIII

## A FINAL SONNET

*for Chris*

How strange to be gone in a minute!     A man
Signs a shovel and so he digs     Everything
Turns into writing a name for a day
                                        Someone
is having a birthday and someone is getting
married and someone is telling a joke     my dream
a white tree     I dream of the code of the west
But this rough magic I here abjure     and
When I have required some heavenly music     which even now
I do     to work mine end upon *their* senses
That this aery charm is for     I'll break
My staff     bury it certain fathoms in the earth
And deeper than did ever plummet sound
I'll drown my book.
It is 5:15 a.m.                    Dear Chris, hello.

# NOTES

MS refers throughout to a typescript of *The Sonnets* in its entirety, from circa 1963, on which Berrigan made notes in September of 1982. Items in quotation marks are annotations to that manuscript made by Berrigan in 1982. Occasionally, earlier changes appear in the manuscript, made before the "C" Press edition of *The Sonnets*, and are indicated as such.

## I (p. 1)
The author often said that the unnamed figure in this sonnet is Ezra Pound. Cf "The End" (first published in *Red Wagon*), written after Pound's death in 1971, which likewise refers to Pound only as "he": "You who are the class in the sky, receive him / Into where you dwell. May he rest long and well / God help him, he invented us, that is, a future / Open living beneath his spell . . ."

## II (p. 2)
Margie: Margie Kepler, a nurse, who was a friend of Berrigan's in Tulsa.

"How Much Longer Shall I Be Able To Inhabit The Divine": "How much longer shall I be able to inhabit the divine sepulcher of life, my great love" is the title and first line of a poem by John Ashbery in *The Tennis Court Oath*.

## III (p. 3)
In MS there is a dedication *"Homage to Arthur Rimbaud."* Cf Sonnet LXX.

## V (p. 5)
MS: "These 5 were done in one sitting, one evening circa Feb 63"—i.e., the first five sonnets.

## VI (p. 6)

MS: "Probably these first VI made in the one night. from lines by Dick, from several poems. The method is similar in all." That is, in fact, all of the first six were probably made in one night, and this sonnet is made from lines by Dick Gallup.

## "Poem In the Traditional Manner" (p. 7)

MS: "(Horatio St.) (inserted here because next one already existed)." That is, the poem was written in Ted's apartment at 81 Horatio Street. It was written after the next poem, "Poem In the Modern Manner," to be its companion piece.

The poem is dated November 1961 in MS, making it one of the poems written previous to the spring of 1963.

Richard Gallup: Dick Gallup (b. 1941) the American poet and close friend of Berrigan in Tulsa and New York. Called Richard here in an allusion to the poem "Richard Cory" by Edward Arlington Robinson.

## "Poem In the Modern Manner" (p. 8)

In MS the poem is dedicated to Ron Padgett and dated December 1961. The author's comment is "(inserted here—given to me on Horatio St. by Ron as discarded poem, lots of other work—for me to 'work on.'" That is, this poem and the previous one are poems made in a similar manner from friends' discarded works.

Huitzilopochtli: Aztec god of war, who had a hideous countenance and to whom human sacrifice was made.

Cos: The Greek island.

## "From a Secret Journal" (p. 9)

MS: "Made from Joe's 'Secret Journal', a prose work, by method. probably made earlier—62 or not? my best." Joe is, of course, Joe Brainard.

## "Real Life" (p. 10)

MS contains the annotation "2 for Bernie Mitchell." The first poem is dated "Nov or so 1961." At the bottom of the second are three comments: "much earlier 1961—maybe Feb"; "(2 older poems, from Horatio St, Oct or Nov 61 inserted here)"; "#'s VII to XII 'selected' i.e. 'made' about a week after first 6, so probably March 63."

Bernie: Bernie Mitchell, sister of Patricia (Pat, Patsy) Mitchell Padgett.

## "Penn Station" (p. 11)

In MS comes before "Real Life" and "Sonnet X" is written by hand above the title. Also has a dedication "for Patsy Nicholson," who was a friend of Ted's in Tulsa.

And near the dedication: "Any one with title got written that way, but was still the sonnet of next #." That is, each titled sonnet also has an unwritten number in the sequence.

Below the poem is the note: "Apr 63? (maybe moved back a bit chronologically to here in final version." And: "This has an actual event in it—the 1963 St. Patrick's Day Parade—probably home a few days later."

The word "Gomangani" is asterisked, with the following footnote: "either White Ape (Tarzan) or Black Apes (The Apes) hence, I forget—i.e. clarity is in the language not its precision." The reference, that is, is to the Tarzan books of Edgar Rice Burroughs.

In MS in line 12 the "mien florist" is the "mean florist." The word was changed for the "C" Press edition.

### XIII (p. 12)
MS: "late night, probably a day later or two after preceding 1 prob late Apr. (TC Oath influence)."

### XIV (p. 13)
One of the sonnets included for the first time in this edition.

MS: "probably next day—using A Lily For My Love (by me) as method and source(/) free use of method (/) end of April." *A Lily For My Love* was Berrigan's first book, published in a small edition in Providence in 1959.

Some words are crossed out in the last two lines of the old version with the notation "This change made 16 Sept '82."

"Blake-blues" probably refers to Blind Blake, the blues guitarist (b. early 1890s, d. 1933).

### XV (p. 14)
MS: "probably written straight out end of April, 1, 2 or 3 of May, '63 lines rearranged by arithmetical formula

    Line  1
          14
           2
          13
           3
          12
         etc.

The only one in the book that can be reconstituted" (cf Sonnet LIX, which is the reconstituted version).

Joe Brainard (1942–1994): American painter, collagist, assemblagist, and poet, who was a close friend of Berrigan's in Tulsa and New York. The collage described here is now in the Joe Brainard Archive at the University of California at San Diego.

### XVI (p. 15)
The poem is dated 4 May 63 in MS: "Arthurian Ashbery at The Antarctic! Free improvisation & method using collaboration by me and Ron written maybe in March or early April. 'The Going Down of the Morning Land' is how Lauren Owen's father translated 'The Decline of the West' to me in 1960 in Tulsa—*slow* was my word."

### XVII (p. 16)
Dated 4 May 63 in MS. The typescript contains an initial different line arrangement, with pencil directions for the arrangement of lines as it stood in the "C" Press edition and subsequently.

In margin (from Sept '82): "Whiteheadean [illegible]."

At the bottom of the page, "this (in re-typed version)" with arrow toward the date of composition. And "A direct 'variation' on an Ashbery poem in *Some Trees*, it's rearranged—used both ways, but with the method rearrangement first." The poem by Ashbery is "Sonnet" ("Each servant stamps the reader with a look").

Carol Clifford: Close friend of Berrigan's, married to Dick Gallup.

### XVIII (p. 17)
In MS dated 4 May 63: "insertion of poem from circa Feb 1961, 210 E. 6th St between 2nd & 3rd storefront with Joe" and: "a method rearrangement."

Larry Walker, David Bearden, and Martin Cochran had all been friends in Tulsa.

### XIX (p. 18)
Next to line 6 on MS: "Rory Calhoun." Rory Calhoun was a movie star, active in the 1950s, who specialized in roles in black-and-white Westerns.

Line 10 has an asterisk with the note: "see *The Sweet Science* by A. J. Liebling." In that book, in a passage about Jack Kearns, a manager of famous boxers, Liebling writes:

> . . . Kearns had the fortune to meet the two fighters who in my opinion had the best ring names of all time—Honey Mellody and Mysterious Billy Smith. Smith was also a welterweight champion. "He was always doing something

mysterious," Kearns says. "Like he would step on your foot, and when you looked down, he would bite you in the ear. If I had a fighter like that now, I could lick heavyweights. . . ." (*The Sweet Science*, page 69)

At the bottom: "1st version May 4th, 1963—rearranged on 6 June 63." In the lower-right-hand corner: "FOH at The Palace (in the movies." FOH is Frank O'Hara. In "Sonnet Workshop" in *On the Level, Everyday*, Berrigan says, "I used to go to a theater called the Palace Theater. It had plush seats, and the experience was sort of like a dark trance in the trembling afternoon."

### XXI (p. 19)
In MS dated 4 May 63: "method re-arrangement of Penn Station inserted here." The poem contains all the lines of "Penn Station" but in an entirely different arrangement. The first five lines are of an ordering similar to that used to make XV, that is proceeding from first line to last line, second line, second to last line, and on inward, but after the fifth line that order stops. The poem ends, though, with what had been line 8 in "Penn Station": it has still managed to turn that poem inside out.

### XXII (p. 20)
Originally dated 6 May 63 in MS, the sonnet has been revised and dated first Sept 16, 82 and then "re-arranged the 27 Sept 82." It appears here for the first time.

### XXIII (p. 21)
In MS dated 12 May 63, with comment at bottom: "breakthrough." This beautiful sonnet elevates the series to the higher plane of artistry and feeling that characterizes the middle and end of the book.

"Between Oologah and Pawnee" (two towns in Oklahoma) is an allusion to the poem "Annie," by Guillaume Apollinaire, which contains the phrase *"Entre Mobile et Galveston."*

### XXV (p. 22)
Printed for the first time here. MS: "False lead / failed poem, tho method nearly carried it—not enough feeling for the words"; then "now fixed (26 Sept 82."

*The Asiatics*: a novel by Frederick Prokosch, first published in 1935.

### XXVI (p. 23)
In MS dated "8,9 May": "see line 1: This sex I meant to be a love night and real, whispered I, etc        Made up by me—a poem written in phonetics, tho wanting

to convey not an inside message, but via surface—i.e.—women will betray you, why—etc. no conclusion."

## XXVII (p. 24)
In MS, in line 11, the word "technically" has been crossed out and replaced with "stealthily," change made circa 1963–64.

## XXVIII (p. 25)
This sonnet is published here for the first time.

## XXIX (p. 26)
In MS dated 14 May 63, this sonnet is published here for the first time. The original poem has been revised (September 1982) mostly by rearranging the lines.

Okinawa was the site of one of the bloodiest campaigns of World War II.

## XXXI (p. 28)
This poem shows the influence of Kenneth Koch, whose poem "You Were Wearing" contains the line "I smelled the mould of your seaside resort hotel bedroom on your hair held in place by a John Greenleaf Whittier clip." Cf Sonnet XL and other sonnets referring to "the Jay Kenneth Koch movie, *Phooey!*" (a reference to a dream of Berrigan's).

In "Sonnets Workshop," in *On the Level, Everyday*, Berrigan says, " 'The boats' was a particularly horrifying form of death, punishment by death, slow death."

## XXXIII (p. 30)
Published here for the first time, this sonnet is dated 21 May 63 in MS. It was revised in September 1982 not by line rearrangement but by changes in punctuation and line endings and the addition of a very few words.

## XXXIV (p. 31)
In MS dated 21 May 63, this sonnet was restored in the United Artists Edition.

Sonnets XXXIV, LXXVII, and LXXXI were actually first published in *Red Wagon* in a context also including three previously published sonnets. This nonsequential arrangement of the six sonnets into an untitled group is an example of Berrigan's continuing interest in the poems as movable parts of space-time and in the ongoing applicability of their method. Cf, for example, "Three Sonnets and a Coda for Tom Clark" (also in *Red Wagon*), which applies the method of *The Sonnets* (minus repetition) to lines from *In the Early Morning Rain*.

**XXXV (p. 32)**

In MS dated 21 May 63. In line 7 "but came rarely" was originally "but rarely came."

Restored in United Artists Edition.

**XXXVI (p. 33)**

In MS dated "28 July 1962."

Lorenz and Ellen Gude were the publishers of Berrigan's "C" Magazine and of the first edition of *The Sonnets*.

Uijongbu: A town in Korea where Berrigan was stationed during his military service.

**XXXVII (p. 34)**

In MS dated 23 May 63.

**XXXVIII (p. 35)**

In MS dated 24 May 63.

Ticonderoga was the site of an American victory in the Revolutionary War in which Benedict Arnold and Ethan Allen led the Continental Army in the capture of the fort from the British.

"A man signs a shovel / And so he digs": reference to Marcel Duchamp's first American ready-made, a snow shovel purchased at a hardware store that Duchamp signed and entitled, writing the words thereon, "In Advance of the Broken Arm."

**"Mess Occupations" (p. 36)**

In MS dated 28 May 63. A "phonetic translation" of Henri Michaux's poem *"Mes Occupations."*

**XL (p. 37)**

In MS dated 28 May 63.

**XLI (p. 38)**

In MS dated 1 June 63.

Ira Hayes (1923–1955), Pima Indian war hero, was one of the five or six U.S. Marines who raised the American flag on Mount Suribachi, Iwo Jima, in 1945. The raising of the flag was the subject of a famous photograph, and Hayes became depressed by all the attendant publicity. He returned to the Pima reservation in Arizona and died of alcoholism and exposure.

## XLII (p. 39)
In MS dated 1 June 63.

## XLIV (p. 41)
In MS dated 1 June 63.

Anne: Anne Kepler, Margie Kepler's cousin, a musician who came to New York from Tulsa around the same time as Berrigan, Brainard, Padgett, and Gallup. She died in 1965, of smoke poisoning, in a fire set by an arsonist, as stated in Berrigan's poem "People Who Died."

## XLV (p. 42)
In MS dated 1 June 63.

## XLVI (p. 43)
Lauren Owen: A friend of Berrigan's in Tulsa and New York.

## XLVII (p. 44)
William Bonney was the real name of Billy the Kid.

## XLVIII (p. 45)
Francis Marion, also known as the Swamp Fox, was a Revolutionary War leader who specialized in guerrilla tactics.

## L (p. 47)
In MS dated 2 June 63.

## LI (p. 48)
In MS dated 6 June 63. At the beginning of line 12 the word "are" has been crossed out and replaced with "and O I am." In line 13 a period has been inserted after "street" and "flushed" changed to "flushing," i.e., the line originally read, "in the street rain flushed the gutters bringing from Memphis." And in the last line "to gulp" is a change from "gulping." These were all changes made before the "C" Press edition.

Gus Cannon (1883–1979), famous banjoist, jug player, and songwriter. He wrote the song "Walk Right In," quoted from in a later poem of Berrigan's, "Things To Do In Anne's Room."

## LII (p. 49)
In MS dated 6 June 63. An early epigraph has been crossed out that reads, "an empty doorway and a maple leaf."

Richard White: American poet whom Berrigan knew in Tulsa and with whom he discussed the works of Charles Olson. Hence the reference in this sonnet to Charles Olson's essay, "Human Universe."

### LIII (p. 49)
This sonnet, dated 6 June 63, originally had the title "Ars Poetica," with the epigraph, "for all the history of grief . . . . ." (thank god that was cut out).

Patsy Padgett, née Patricia Mitchell, was a close friend of Berrigan's in Tulsa and New York.

### LV (p. 51)
In MS dated 8 June 63.

### LVI (p. 52)
In MS dated 8 June 63.

### LVII (p. 53)
In MS dated 9 June 63.

### LIX (p. 54)
Published for the first time as one of the sonnets here, this poem was included on its own in *So Going Around Cities*. Cf Sonnet XV.

### LX (p. 55)
Originally dated November 1962 in MS, the year has been changed by hand to 1961, presumably in September 1982. The sonnet here has the dedication "for Joe Brainard & Pat Mitchell." At the bottom of the page the note: "while Joe made his self-portrait from little pieces of cut-out pages from Life Mag, I cut up in one morning a poem and made this using every piece. at 81 Horatio St."

Ron Padgett: The American poet, translator, and editor, and close friend of the author in Tulsa and New York.

Restored in United Artists Edition.

### LXI (p. 56)
Dated 17 June 1963.

In MS line 12, "in the crevices in my window," reads "in the crevices around my windows."

Big Bill Broonzy (1893–1958), the Chicago blues great, guitarist and vocalist.

Restored in United Artists Edition.

**LXIV (p. 57)**
In MS dated 19 June 63.

**LXV (p. 58)**
In MS dated 19 June 63.

**LXVI (p. 59)**
In MS dated 20 June 63.

**LXVII (p. 60)**
In MS dated 20 June 63.

Chris: Christine Murphy. In 1958–59 Berrigan taught the eighth grade at Mada-lene School in Tulsa. Christine Murphy was one of his students: the two con-ceived an intense (platonic, or at least unconsummated) affection for each other. Christine Murphy is also the "Chris" in the unpublished prose work of Berrigan's, *Looking for Chris*, though not the "Chris" in the poem "Living With Chris" (first pub-lished in *Many Happy Returns*), who is Christina Gallup, the (then) baby daughter of Dick and Carol Gallup.

**LXVIII (p. 61)**
In MS dated 21 June 63.

**LXX (p. 62)**
In MS dated 21 June 63. Cf Sonnet III. The poem is an adaptation of Rimbaud's *"Le Bateau Ivre."*

**LXXI (p. 63)**
In MS dated 23 June 63.

**LXXII (p. 64)**
In MS dated 23 June 63.

**LXXIII (p. 65)**
In MS dated 24 June 63.

**LXXIV (p. 66)**
In MS dated 24 June 63.

**LXXV (p. 67)**
In MS dated November 1961.

**LXXVI (p. 68)**
In MS dated 15 November 1961, Berrigan's twenty-seventh birthday. The poem has a dedication in the typescript, "after Frank O'Hara," which wasn't used in any of the editions of *The Sonnets*.

The phrase "this morning" was apparently originally left off the end of the last line: it has been appended by hand in MS.

**LXXVII (p. 69)**
Had been originally dated February 1962, which has been changed to "February 1961?"

Restored in United Artists Edition.

**LXXVIII (p. 70)**
In MS dated 25 June 63.

**LXXX (p. 71)**
In MS dated 27 June 63.

Louis Sullivan (1856–1924), major American architect. Cf the poem "String of Pearls" in *Nothing For You*. Its last three lines are "climbing the steps of the only major statement in New York City / (Louis Sullivan) thinking the poem I am going to write    seeing / the fountains come on    wishing I were he." "String of Pearls" was written in 1962. The building referred to is probably the Bayard Building on Bleecker Street in Manhattan.

**LXXXI (p. 72)**
In MS dated 28 June 63.

Huddie Ledbetter: Real name of the folksinger Leadbelly (1885–1949).

Lonnie Johnson (1894–1970), considered by some to be the first great modern blues guitarist. According to Ron Padgett, in a letter to Alice Notley: ". . . Ted saw Johnson perform at Folk City in the early 1960s and was quite bowled over by him. There was a great moment when, near the end of a long set, Victoria Spivey leaped onto the bandstand wearing a tight white dress covered with dark rubber snakes and did several stunning numbers with Johnson."

Hans Hoffman: Hans Hofmann (1880–1966), American Abstract Expressionist, influential painter and teacher. His theory of "push-pull" has sometimes been cited in connection with *The Sonnets*; it explores the tension between picture planes, as exemplified in various of his own paintings containing large squares. The word "block" in its various usages throughout *The Sonnets* refers always in part to Hofmann's work.

Restored in United Artists Edition.

**LXXXII (p. 73)**
In MS dated 28 June 63.

**LXXXIII (p. 74)**
In MS dated 29 June 63.

**LXXXIV (p. 75)**
In MS dated 29 June 63.

The last line originally (before the "C" Press edition) read "Even if it does choke you up, and these marvelous tears appear": the "keep" and "ing" have been added by hand here circa 1963–64.

**LXXXV (p. 76)**

In MS dated 29 June 63.

**LXXXVII (p. 77)**
In MS dated 1 July 63.

**LXXXVIII (p. 78)**
In MS dated 7 July 63. The dedication "for Chris" is missing, though it appears in the "C" Press edition.

The clause "someone is telling a joke" originally (before the "C" Press edition) read, "someone is telling jokes."

In the second to last line, "Dear Chris, hello" was at first "Dear Sandy, hello" and then "Dear Margie, hello."

The last line originally read, "Outside my room it is 5:15 a.m." The first three words have been crossed out here establishing the final version.

At the bottom of the page the note, from 1982 below the typewritten date 7 July 63: "Prov RI—David Berrigan born 9 July 63 Prov. RI" (David Berrigan being the author's oldest child).

# PRINCIPAL BOOKS USED
## IN INTRODUCTION AND NOTES

Ashbery, John. 1977. *Some Trees*. New York: The Ecco Press.

Ashbery, John. 1962. *The Tennis Court Oath*. Middletown, CT: Wesleyan University Press.

Berrigan, Ted. 1959. *A Lily For My Love*. Providence: Privately published.

————. 1964. *The Sonnets*. New York: "C" Press.

————. 1966. *The Sonnets*, 2nd edition. New York: Grove Press.

————. 1970. *In the Early Morning Rain*. London: Cape Goliard Press.

————. 1976. *Red Wagon*. Chicago: The Yellow Press.

————. 1977. *Nothing For You*. Lenox, MA: Angel Hair Books.

————. 1980. *So Going Around Cities: New & Selected Poems 1958–1979*. Berkeley: Blue Wind Press.

————. 1982. *The Sonnets*, 3rd edition. New York: United Artists.

————. 1997. *On the Level, Everyday: Selected Talks on Poetry and the Art of Living*. Jersey City: Talisman House, Publishers.

Cage, John. 1973. *Silence*. Middletown, CT: Wesleyan University Press.

Liebling, A. J. 1983. *The Sweet Science*. New York: Penguin.

Motherwell, Robert. 1951. *The Dada Painters and Poets: An Anthology*. New York: Wittenborn.

Tomkins, Calvin, and the Editors of Time-Life Books. 1972. *The World of Marcel Duchamp*. New York: Time-Life Books.

Whitehead, Alfred North. 1979. *Process and Reality*. New York: The Free Press.

# ABOUT THE AUTHOR

Ted Berrigan, poetic and inspirational genius of the second generation of the New York School Poets, was born in Providence, Rhode Island, on November 15, 1934. He was educated at La Salle Academy in Providence and, after sixteen months in Korea as a soldier, at the University of Tulsa (on the GI Bill). During the 1960s he lived in New York's Lower East Side, writing city poems, publishing the exciting and unique "C" Magazine and "C" Press books, writing art criticism, and playing leader to a group of young poets and appreciators of poetry. Later he was Writer In Residence, Lecturer, Teaching Fellow, etc., at such places as The Writers Workshop (University of Iowa), the University of Michigan at Ann Arbor, Yale, State University of New York at Buffalo, the University of Essex (England), Northeastern Illinois University (Chicago), and the Naropa Institute. In the mid-1970s he returned to the Lower East Side, teaching at Stevens Institute of Technology and the City College of New York, giving poetry readings everywhere, and influencing a new generation of poets. His many books include the major sequence *The Sonnets*, a central collection *So Going Around Cities*, several collaborative books with other poets, long poems, a novel, and interviews. In a curriculum vitae from 1982, he described himself as "modestly venerable, large, traditional in appearence. Resemble Apollinaire (w/beard) or bear disguised as GBS . . . Formidable, affable, durable . . ." He died on July 4, 1983.

# PENGUIN POETS

| | |
|---|---|
| Ted Berrigan | *Selected Poems* |
| Ted Berrigan | *The Sonnets* |
| Philip Booth | *Lifelines* |
| Philip Booth | *Pairs* |
| Jim Carroll | *Fear of Dreaming* |
| Jim Carroll | *Void of Course* |
| Nicholas Christopher | *5° & Other Poems* |
| Diane di Prima | *Loba* |
| Stuart Dischell | *Evenings and Avenues* |
| Stephen Dobyns | *Common Carnage* |
| Stephen Dobyns | *Pallbearers Envying the One Who Rides* |
| Paul Durcan | *A Snail in My Prime* |
| Amy Gerstler | *Crown of Weeds* |
| Amy Gerstler | *Medicine* |
| Amy Gerstler | *Nerve Storm* |
| Debora Greger | *Desert Fathers, Uranium Daughters* |
| Robert Hunter | *Glass Lunch* |
| Robert Hunter | *Sentinel* |
| Barbara Jordan | *Trace Elements* |
| Jack Kerouac | *Book of Blues* |
| Ann Lauterbach | *And For Example* |
| Ann Lauterbach | *On a Stair* |
| William Logan | *Night Battle* |
| William Logan | *Vain Empires* |
| Derek Mahon | *Selected Poems* |
| Michael McClure | *Huge Dreams: San Francisco and Beat Poems* |
| Michael McClure | *Three Poems* |
| Carol Muske | *An Octave Above Thunder* |
| Alice Notley | *The Descent of Alette* |
| Alice Notley | *Mysteries of Small Houses* |
| Lawrence Raab | *The Probable World* |
| Anne Waldman | *Kill or Cure* |
| Anne Waldman | *Marriage: A Sentence* |
| Rachel Wetzsteon | *Home and Away* |
| Philip Whalen | *Overtime: Selected Poems* |
| Robert Wrigley | *In the Bank of Beautiful Sins* |
| Robert Wrigley | *Reign of Snakes* |